PEOPLE IN COSTUME

The Romans

JENNIFER RUBY

B.T. Batsford Ltd · London

First published 1995

Typeset by Goodfellow & Egan Ltd, Cambridge

and printed in Hong Kong by Colorcraft

Published by
B.T. Batsford Ltd
4 Fitzhardinge Street
London W1H 0AH

A CIP catalogue record for this book is available from
the British Library

ISBN 0 7134 7621 4

CONTENTS

INTRODUCTION

When the Romans first arrived in Britain they thought it was a wild and uncivilized place. They were used to grand public buildings made of marble and houses with central heating. They were interested in art, philosophy and history. To the Romans, the Celtic people who lived in Britain seemed like savages because they lived in mud huts and could not read or write. The conquest of Britain took place over many years and involved many battles and skirmishes.

The Romans were in Britain for over 350 years. They built the first towns, set up lawcourts and enforced justice. They built beautiful houses, temples and public baths and constructed long, straight roads. In this book you will see different characters from Roman Britain so that you can learn about the clothes they used to wear. First of all, let us meet a centurion.

'Hello, my name is Caius and I am a centurion in the Roman army. This means that I am in charge of 80 men. My armour and equipment are very sophisticated and were manufactured in various different factories in Europe. My helmet fastens under my chin and the ties often cut my skin if I wear it for a long time. The plume on the top goes from left to right rather than front to back to show that I am a centurion and so that my men can spot me easily on the battlefield. My chest armour is put on like a waistcoat and ties in the front. My leather belt is reinforced with metal plates. Underneath all this I am wearing a tunic.

Now I am going to take you on a journey back in time to Roman Britain so that you can learn about the clothes people used to wear.'

AD 43-60: INVASION

Caius

THE CATUVELLAUNI TRIBE

There were many different tribes living in Britain, some of which banded together to try and stop the Roman invasion.

This is Marganus who is a member of the Catuvellauni tribe. He is wearing a soft woollen cap, a striped cloak and stockings. His shoes are made of leather. Like the other Catuvellauni men, he wears his hair long and has a droopy moustache.

Marganus

His wife Imogen is wearing a separate bodice and skirt made of wool. Her hair is long and has a fringe. Celtic people made very beautiful ornaments and jewellery. Imogen is holding a bronze mirror that was made by Marganus. She is also wearing a brooch on her bodice front. You can see more Celtic jewellery on page 44.

Imogen

A LEGIONARY

Alexander

military sandals (caligae) with iron hobnails on the soles were designed to take weight and survive many miles of marching

the tunic was made from two pieces of material stitched together with slits left for the neck and arms

This is Alexander. He is a legionary in the Roman army and will fight Marganus in battle.

He is wearing his armour over a tunic and is carrying his woollen cloak, a water bottle and a pack containing three days rations.

His shield is made from wood and is protected by a leather covering when he is not in battle. His javelin has a specially-designed point which bends when it is pulled out of an enemy's shield. Alexander has a stabbing sword at his right side and wears a dagger at his left.

dagger with double-edged blade

TWO TRIBE LEADERS

Alexander will also meet Caractacus on the battlefield. Caractacus is the leader of the Catuvellauni tribe.

Caractacus is a warrior and is wearing a helmet made from leather and bronze. The horns on the top are hollow. His tunic is made from checked material and he has a fine belt at his waist. His loose trousers are called braies and his shoes are made of leather. Around his neck he is wearing a gold torque* which shows that he is a man of high rank.

Caractacus fought bravely in battle but eventually he was captured and taken to Rome. Can you find out more about him?

Caractacus

* A torque is a necklace made from twisted metal.

Boudicca

This is Boudicca (or Boadicea), the queen of the Iceni tribe in Norfolk. She led a revolt against the Romans.

Her people have a good knowledge of weaving, spinning and dyeing. She is wearing a gown made from thick, coarse cloth which has been dyed in reds and greens. She is also wearing a woollen cloak and leather shoes and belt. She has a mane of long red hair.

The name Boudicca means 'Victory'. Can you discover what happened to her?

AD 150: VERULAMIUM

We will now move forward to the year AD 150 and visit the Roman city of Verulamium.

This is Lucius Antistius who is a senator. This means that he helps in the government of the city.

He is wearing a simple white tunic with a belt at the waist and leather boots. His tunic has a purple stripe down the front to show that he is a senator. His hair has been curled and he is clean-shaven.

When he goes out, Lucius wears a toga. This is a kind of cloak made from a semicircular piece of material. It is very large, and Lucius wears it in complicated folds and drapes over his body.

Lucius

5.5 m

2.2 m

the toga was folded
from a semicircular
piece of cloth 5.5 m
long

TWO SLAVES

Lucius Antistius has many slaves working for him in his beautiful villa. Anthus works closely with Lucius, helping him with his clothes and his toilet preparations.

Anthus is wearing a woollen tunic with a belt at the waist and leather sandals.

Julia works in the kitchen. She is wearing a stola. This is a long, sleeveless gown, rather like a tunic in shape. It is secured at her waist with a belt.

The law allowed slave owners to treat their slaves how they wished. Some slaves were paid wages and sometimes they managed to save enough to buy their freedom.

Anthus

Julia

THE SENATOR'S WIFE

This is Lucius's wife Modestina. She is wearing a stola which she has decorated with large jewelled brooches on her shoulders. She is also wearing a jewelled necklace. Two different kinds of footwear from her wardrobe are pictured below.

When she goes out, Modestina wears a palla over her stola. This is a large cloak, rather like the toga, which she drapes over her body. It is made of wool. She is wearing one in the picture opposite and she also has a kerchief on her head.

Modestina

leather sandal

soft leather slipper

You can see that Roman women wore very simple clothes. The beauty of their costumes came from the way the fabric was draped and the jewellery that they wore. Gold neck-laces, bracelets and rings were often worn, and these were decorated with precious gems like emeralds, opals, pearls and rubies. You can see more jewellery on pages 44 and 45.

Women tended to prefer lighter materials than men. Instead of wool they liked to wear soft cotton from India and they especially liked silks. Dyers coloured them in light or dark blues, yellows or reds. Sea-green, azure-blue and flesh-pink were also popular colours.

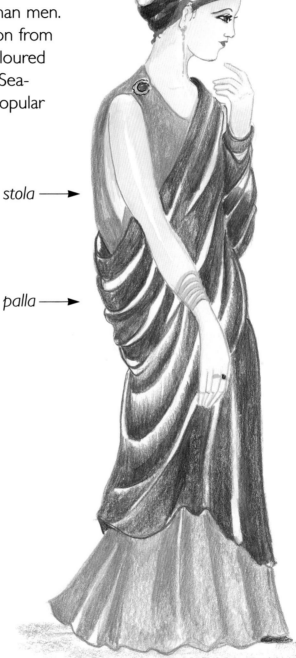

stola ⟶

palla ⟶

IN THE KITCHEN

Here is Julia coming out of the kitchen with a plate of food for her master and mistress. She is wearing a shawl draped over her stola and around her hips.

On the right Servillius, another slave, is busily chopping vegetables for a banquet in the evening. He is wearing a woollen tunic and leather sandals.

Lucius and Modestina tend to eat little during the day, but they have a large meal in the evening. Tonight, at the banquet, they are going to eat dormouse cooked in honey and poppy seed. With this, they will have vegetables and olives. For their dessert they will have fruit, nuts and honey and they will drink large quantities of wine.

Julia

Servillius will help with the cooking of the food. This will be boiled in large pots or grilled. Can you find out more about Roman food and cooking?

Servillius

AT THE FORUM

The forum in a Roman town was a large open space that was used as a market-place. It was surrounded on three sides by covered walkways which contained shops and offices. On the fourth side there was usually a large building which was used as a lawcourt.

The market square is always busy with traders, shoppers and
street entertainers. Amulius is a street trader. He is wearing
a simple woollen tunic and leather boots. He is selling pots
and pans and is talking to Tulia who has come to the forum
to buy some provisions. Tulia is wearing a blue stola. She has
jewellery in her hair and gold bracelets on her wrists.

Amulius

Tulia

IN THE STREET

Further down the market-place we meet Turnus the baker.
He is wearing a tunic with a leather belt around his waist and
leather boots with laces. The two boys are playing the 'mill
game', which is rather like our game of draughts. They are
also wearing tunics.

Turnus

Octavia and Livia are deep in conversation. Both women are wearing stolas which are made from light, flimsy material. Octavia has a thin shawl over her head and shoulders and Livia is wearing a palla.

Livia

Octavia

A VISIT TO THE DOCTOR

Marcus

Under one of the covered walkways we can see Marcus the doctor, tending to a patient at his clinic. Marcus is wearing a long tunic with sleeves.

His patient is a wounded soldier who is wearing a tunic with a belt. He has a cloak slung over his shoulder and his sandals are made of leather.

What do you think is wrong with the small boy in the picture?

Some of Marcus's instruments are pictured below. He often uses herbs for healing. For example, fenugreek is used to treat pneumonia and fennel for calming people down. He also advises his patients to eat garlic to keep them healthy. Other ingredients that go into his pills and potions include rosemary, sage and mustard.

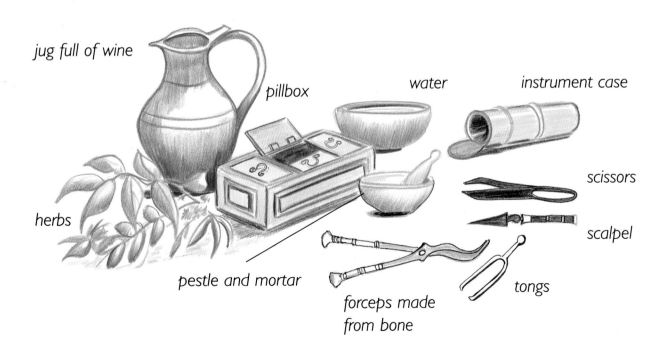

jug full of wine

pillbox

water

instrument case

scissors

scalpel

herbs

pestle and mortar

forceps made from bone

tongs

AT THE AMPHITHEATRE

The Romans loved to go to the amphitheatre to watch the gladiator fights. Gladiators were mostly slaves or criminals and were trained to fight at special schools. There were different types of gladiator who were distinguished by their weapons and costumes.

Celadus is a Samnite. He is wearing a metal helmet which has a flap at the back to protect his neck and flaps at the front to protect his throat. His only clothing is a loin cloth and a leather belt and sandals. His right arm and left thigh are protected with strip armour and he has metal shin protectors. He is carrying a shield and dagger.

Celadus is going to fight the nimble Rufus. Rufus is a retarius or 'net man'. He is equipped like a fisherman with a net to catch his foe.

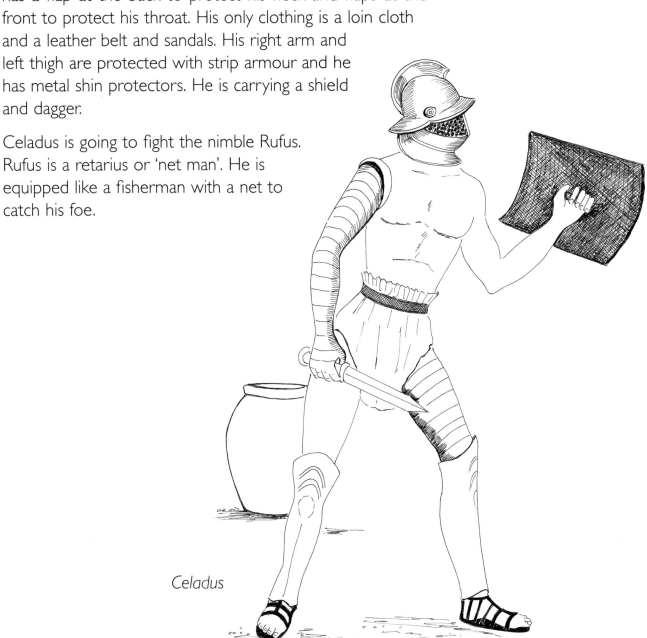

Celadus

Rufus is wearing a tunic held up by a strap over one shoulder and he has a leather belt around his waist. He has strip armour on his left arm and leather sandals on his feet. His weapons are a trident* and a dagger.

Gladiators usually fought to the death, but defeated or wounded fighters could appeal for mercy. The sand in the arena was often coloured so that the blood did not show up so much. There were vats of incense burning to disguise the smell.

Who do you think will win this fight?

Rufus

* A trident is a three-pronged spear.

GOING TO A PLAY

Here is the amphitheatre from the outside. This time it is
being used to stage a play. The theatre holds thousands of
people. Poorer people sit high up, furthest away from the
actors. The best seats are reserved for the senators.

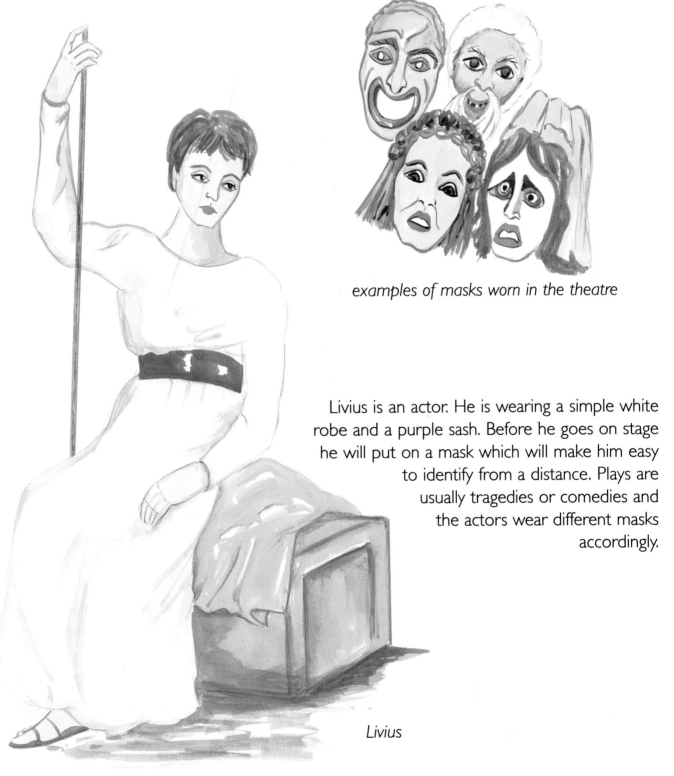

examples of masks worn in the theatre

Livius is an actor. He is wearing a simple white robe and a purple sash. Before he goes on stage he will put on a mask which will make him easy to identify from a distance. Plays are usually tragedies or comedies and the actors wear different masks accordingly.

Livius

29

BACKSTAGE

Julius

Julius is backstage helping Livius with his props. The different masks that Livius wears are made of shaped and stiffened linen. Each mask has a gaping mouth for him to speak through and holes for him to see through. They are very large and can be hot to wear.

Julius is wearing a long sleeved tunic, tied around the middle with a belt.

Can you design some colourful masks for the Roman theatre?

A CHARIOTEER

Sometimes the amphitheatre is used for chariot races. These races are very exciting.

Brutus is a charioteer. He is wearing a tunic and leather sandals. He has ropes tied around his body and thighs to protect him if he should fall.

He has just won a race and is carrying a victor's palm. The prize is a purse of gold. Brutus is a slave and is saving up to buy his freedom.

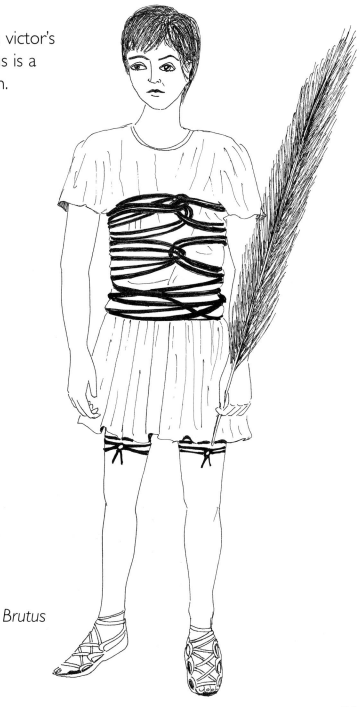

Brutus

A WEDDING

Now we will return to Lucius's house where his eldest daughter Helena is getting married. In Roman times it was the custom for a bride to wear a saffron*-coloured cloak and veil. Helena's veil is worn over six pads and completely hides her brow. For the ceremony she will wear a wreath of marjoram and verbena on her head.

Her two sisters, Sabina and Cassia, are pictured opposite. They are wearing flimsy, almost transparent robes and shawls in beautiful colours. Their hair has been dressed in elaborate curls and decorated with jewels and they are both wearing necklaces and bracelets.

You can see Sabina again on page 40.

*Saffron is an orange-yellow colour.

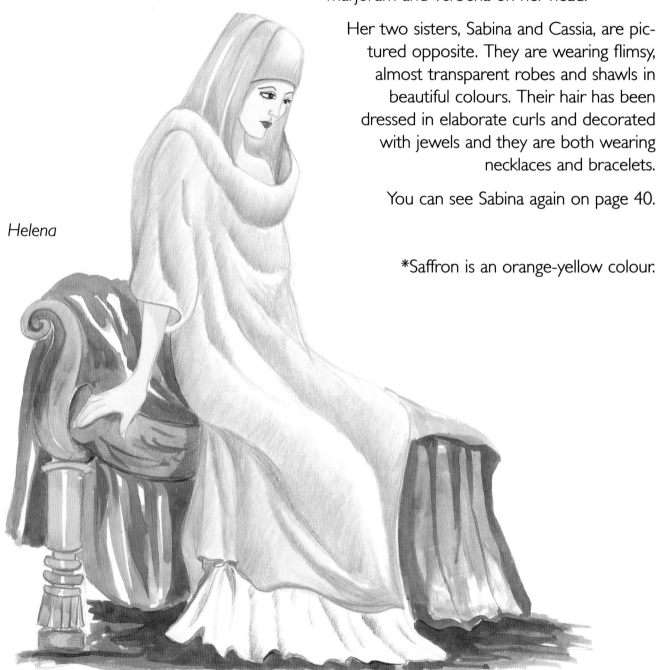

Helena

Cassia

Sabina

ENTERTAINERS

After the ceremony there will be a banquet with music and dancing. Anthony is a musician and he is entertaining the wedding guests by playing a rather strange shaped horn. Sometimes he plays a flute like the one in the picture below. Anthony is wearing a tunic and leather sandals. He has a laurel wreath on his head.

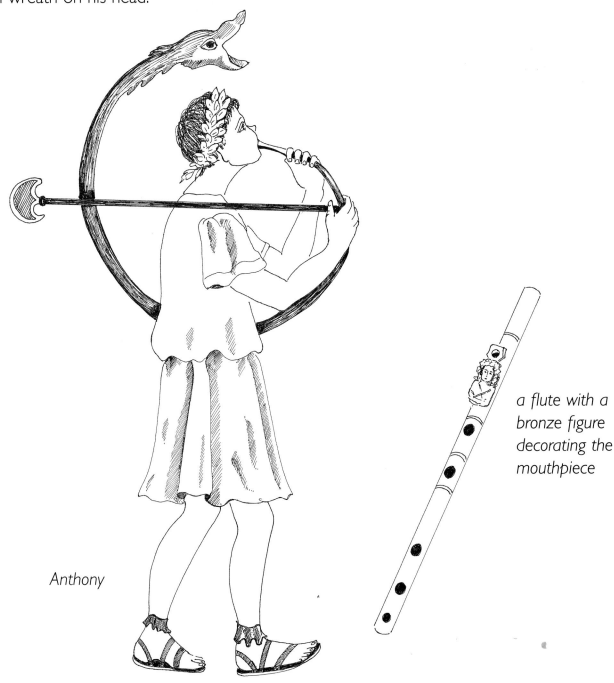

Anthony

a flute with a bronze figure decorating the mouthpiece

Rhea is a slave girl. She is dancing for the guests. Rhea is wearing a stola and a flimsy veil draped over the upper part of her body. However, like all Roman women, she has complemented her simple costume with lots of jewellery.

What other kinds of entertainers might have been at the celebrations?

AT THE BATHS

As few Roman houses had baths, most people went to the large public baths to get clean. Here they would meet their friends, chat, exercise and relax.

Men and women did not bathe together, instead they attended the baths at different times.

Helena often goes to the public baths with her friend Plotina. Both girls like to exercise, bathe and have a massage. Their outfits are very similar to what we would call a bikini. The top half is called a strophium and the lower half a pagne.

As the Romans do not have soap, dirt and sweat are removed by covering the body with oil and then scraping it off with an instrument called a strigil. Helena and Plotina take slave girls with them to help them and to give them massages.

Can you find out more about the Roman baths?

Helena

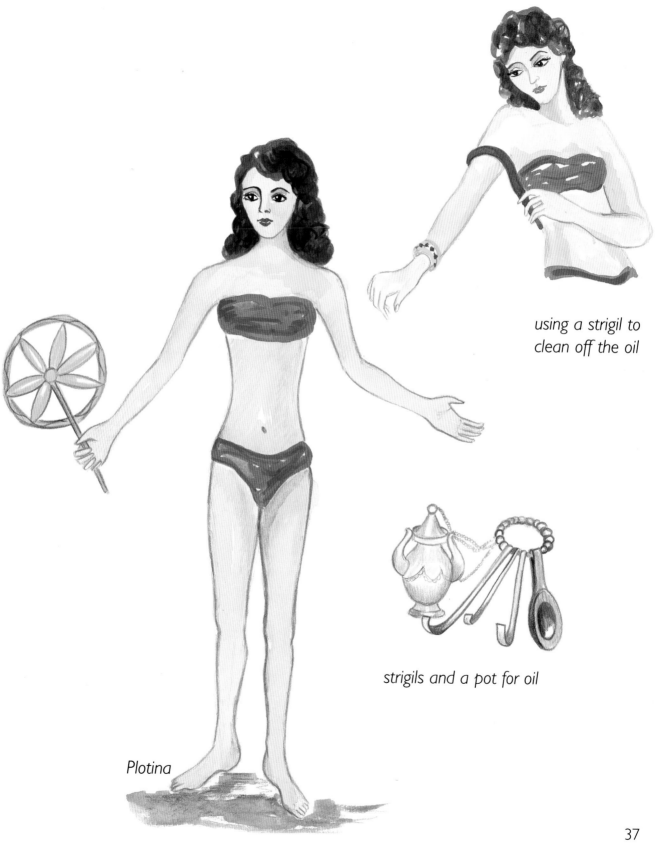

using a strigil to clean off the oil

strigils and a pot for oil

Plotina

AD 450: THE SAXONS

In AD 406 all Roman troops were recalled from Britain to defend Rome. This meant that Britain was almost defenceless against its various enemies. The Saxons, who came from north-west Europe, began to invade and settle in the country.

This is Hengist, a leader of one of the early Saxon invasions. He has decided to stay in Britain with his wife and family.

Hengist is wearing a pointed woollen cap, called a Phrygian cap, and a tunic with sleeves and a decorated border. His baggy trousers are called braies and have been cross-gartered with linen strips from the knees down. His cloak is made of wool and is secured at the front with a jewelled brooch.

Hengist

This is Renwein, Hengist's daughter. Her hair is covered by a head rail. This is a large square of linen material worn over the head and draped over one shoulder. Over this she is wearing a circlet of gold.

Renwein has on two gowns and a cloak (or mantle) on top.

Why do you think she wears so many layers of clothing?

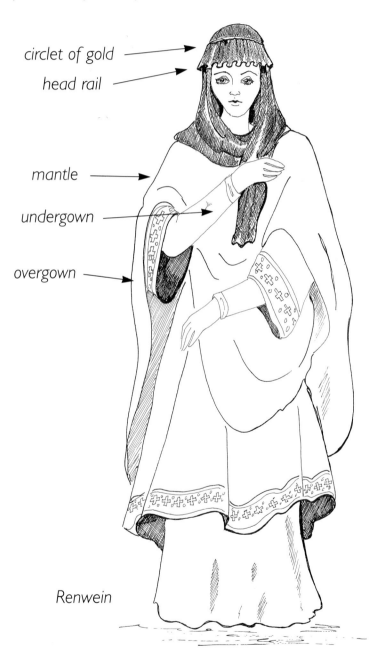

circlet of gold

head rail

mantle

undergown

overgown

Renwein

CHILDREN'S CLOTHES

Children were usually dressed like their parents in Roman times. Here is Sabina, whom you first met on page 33. She is wearing a stola and palla which she has draped over her body and secured with brooches. She is wearing heavy eye make-up and lots of jewellery.

On the right you can see a small Roman boy aged about 8. He is wearing a tunic, toga and leather sandals. His strange curls indicate that his family are worshippers of Isis. Around his neck he is wearing a bulla. This is a charm to ward off evil spirits.

The Saxon boy on the far right is wearing a tunic and braies (baggy trousers) with cross-binding over the top. His shoes are made from leather.

Which of the two boys would be more comfortable in his clothes?

Sabina

COSMETICS

Make-up was very important to Roman women. A pale complexion was fashionable. Powdered chalk or white lead was applied to the face to make it look white (**this is dangerous, so do not try it**), then a little rouge was added to the cheeks. Heavy eye make-up was used, and eyelids were often darkened with ash or a substance called antimony. Black and gold eyeshadows were fashionable.

Wigs and hair dyes were used and flowers were grown to make perfumes which were stored in beautiful scent bottles.

Men often wore make-up too, and frequently ruined their skin by putting poisonous lead on their faces.

Helena is busy mixing some cosmetics. She is wearing a stola and leather sandals and has a veil over her hair.

When you are drawing pictures of Roman women remember to give them heavy eye make-up!

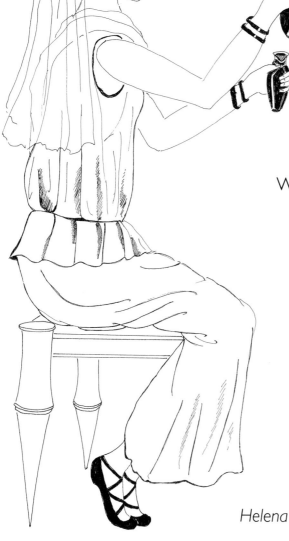

Helena

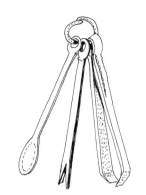

cosmetic set of ear
scoop, nail cleaners
and tweezers

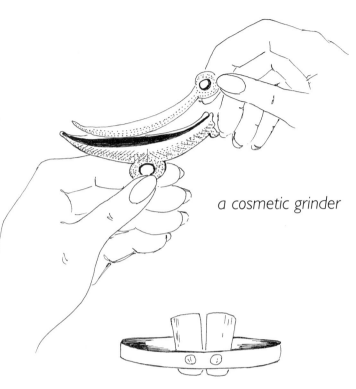

a cosmetic grinder

false teeth – extracted teeth
were riveted to gold bridges

scent bottle carved
from precious onyx

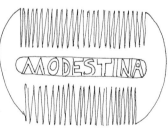

ivory comb

silver spatula for mixing
and applying cosmetics

JEWELLERY

Roman men and women loved to wear jewellery. Rings were very popular and often several were worn on each finger. The middle finger was left bare for superstitious reasons. Necklaces, bracelets and earrings were also fashionable.

gold snake bracelet for the upper arm (Roman)

a bronze belt boss

a bronze pendant that the lady opposite might wear round her neck

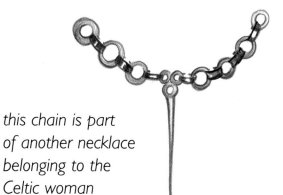

this chain is part of another necklace belonging to the Celtic woman

Celtic woman wearing a neck ring or torque, a bronze belt boss and a spiral bracelet

The Celtic people whom you met at the beginning of the book also made and wore beautiful jewellery. On these two pages you can see examples of some precious items worn by the Celts and Romans.

Roman men and women wore rings set with precious stones

the Romans believed that a gold bracelet shaped like this would bring long life to the wearer

pins like these were carved from ivory or gold and were worn in the hair or pinned to the clothing

a gold bracelet

pearl earrings

A Roman lady wearing pearl earrings and an emerald necklace

gold necklace set with emeralds and pearls

HAIRSTYLES

Roman men and women spent a lot of time on their hair. Men wore their hair quite short but it was carefully curled with hot irons and perfumed. Baldness was considered to be a deformity and if a man was going bald he would wear a wig. The barber's shop was a place to meet friends and to gossip, but being shaved there was often painful. The barber did not use any oil or soap with his sharp razor, so cuts were frequent!

Women had slaves to dress their hair in elaborate curls and plaits. They often wore wigs and hairpieces. Sometimes rich women cut the hair of their slaves in order to make wigs for themselves.

this boy has his hair short and brought forward over his forehead